~A BINGO BOOK~

Japan Bingo Book

COMPLETE BINGO GAME IN A BOOK

Written By Rebecca Stark
Educational Books 'n' Bingo

ISBN 978-0-87386-483-1

Educational Books 'n' Bingo

Printed in the U.S.A.

JAPAN BINGO DIRECTIONS

INCLUDED:

List of Terms

Templates for Additional Terms and Clues

2 Clues per Term

30 Unique Bingo Cards

Markers

1. **Either cut apart the book or make copies of ALL the sheets. You might want to make an extra copy of the clue sheets to use for introduction and review. Keep the sheets in an envelope for easy reuse.**

2. Cut apart the call cards with terms and clues.

3. Pass out one bingo card per student. There are enough for a class of 30.

4. Pass out markers. You may cut apart the markers included in this book or use any other small items of your choice.

5. Decide whether or not you will require the entire card to be filled. Requiring the entire card to be filled provides a better review. However, if you have a short time to fill, you may prefer to have them do the just the border or some other format. Tell the class before you begin what is required.

6. There are 50 terms. Read the list before you begin. If there are any terms that have not been covered in class, you may want to read to the students the term and clues before you begin.

7. There is a blank space in the middle of each card. You can instruct the students to use it as a free space or you can write in answers to cover terms not included. Of course, in this case you would create your own clues. (Templates provided.)

8. Shuffle the cards and place them in a pile. Two or three clues are provided for each term. If you plan to play the game with the same group more than once, you might want to choose a different clue for each game. If not, you may choose to use more than one clue.

9. Be sure to keep the cards you have used for the present game in a separate pile. When a student calls, "Bingo," he or she will have to verify that the correct answers are on his or her card AND that the markers were placed in response to the proper questions. Pull out the cards that are on the student's card keeping them in the order they were used in the game. Read each clue as it was given and ask the student to identify the correct answer from his or her card.

10. If the student has the correct answers on the card AND has shown that they were marked in response to the *correct questions,* then that student is the winner and the game is over. If the student does not have the correct answers on the card OR he or she marked the answers in response to *the wrong questions,* then the game continues until there is a proper winner.

11. If you want to play again, reshuffle the cards and begin again.

Have fun!

TERMS/NAMES

Ainu

Archipelago

Asia

Bakufu

Bonsai

Bow(-ing)

Buddhism

Cherry Tree(s)

Chicamatsu Monzaemon

Chrysanthemum Throne

Daimyo

Diet

Edo

Emperor(s)

Haiku

Hideki Tojo

Hiroshima

Hokkaido

Honshu

Ikebana

Imperial Palace

Kabuki

Kamikaze(s)

Kobe

Kyoto

Matso Basho

Meiji

Minamoto Yoritomo

Mount Fuji

Mount Misen

Nara

Oda Nobunaga

Okinawa

Osaka

Pearl Harbor

Prefectures

Rice

Rim of Fire

Russo-Japanese War

Samurai

Sea of Japan

Shinto

Shogun(s)

Taika Reforms

Tokugawa Ieyasu

Tokyo

Toyotomi Hideyoshi

Tsunami(s)

Wabi-sabi

Yokohama

NOTE: Some names may have alternative spellings.

Japan Bingo

Additional Terms

Choose as many additional terms as you would like and write them in the squares. Repeat each as desired.
Cut out the squares and randomly distribute them to the class.
Instruct the students to place their square on the center space of their card.

Clues for Additional Terms

Write two clues for each of your additional terms.

_____	_____
1.	1.
2.	2.
_____	_____
1.	1.
2.	2.
	.
_____	_____
1.	1.
2.	2.

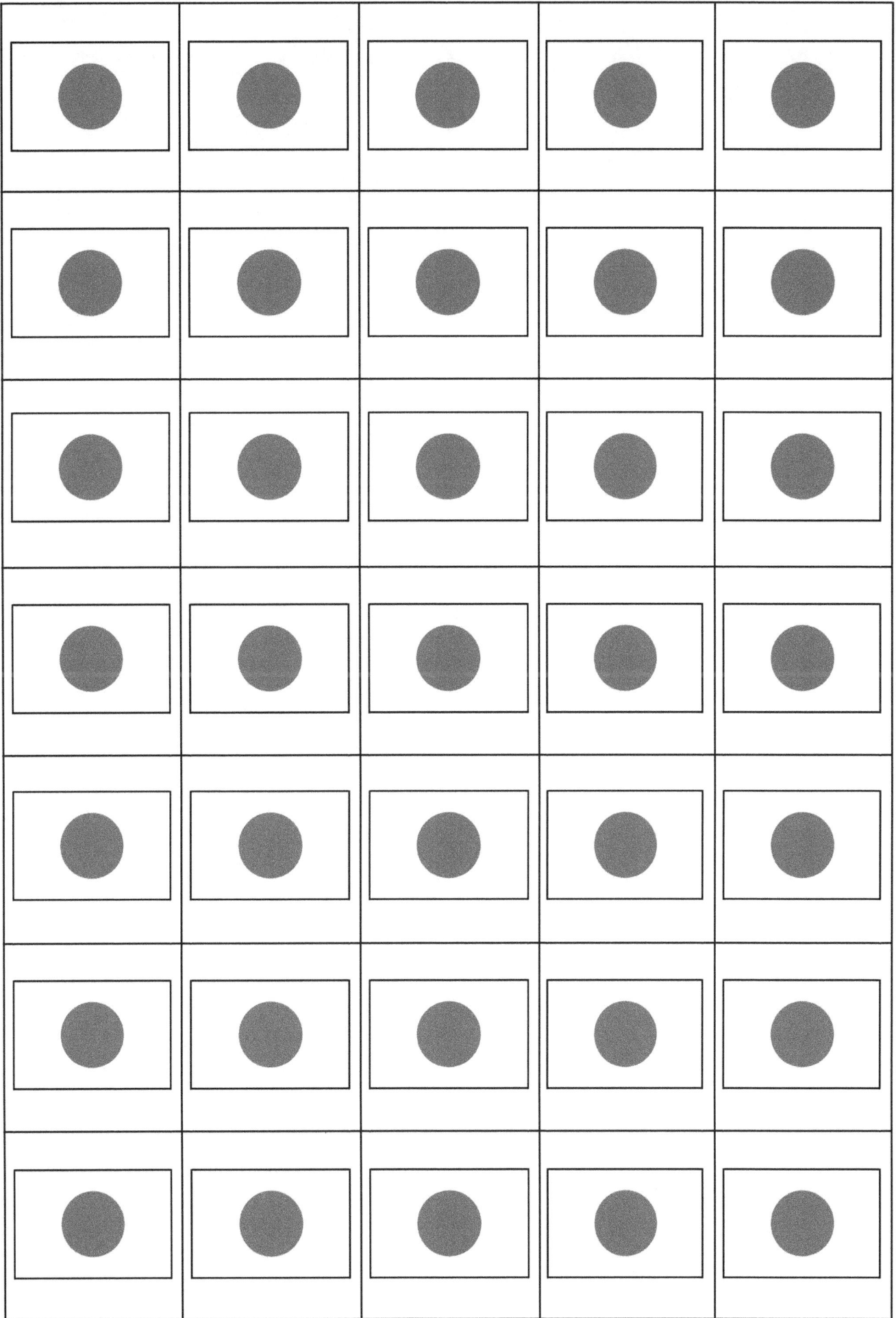

Ainu 1. These native people arrrived by boat from Siberia about 12,000 years ago. 2. The ___ are indigenous people of Japan. The small remaining population lives mainly in Hokkaido.	**Archipelago** 1. Japan is an ___, or chain of islands, in the Pacific Ocean. 2. The Japanese ___ is a string of thousands of islands. The four largest from are Honshu, Hokkaido, Kyushu, and Shikoku. (largest to smallest of the 4)
Asia 1. ___ is the largest continent. 2. ___ is the most populous continent.	**Bakufu** 1. A *shogun's* office or government is also called a ___. 2. Literally, ___ means "tent office." It is another term for *shogunate.*
Bonsai 1. ___ originated in China and is similar to the Chinese art of *penjing.* 2. ___ is the art of growing trees and plants in a pot, kept small and artistically shaped by pruning.	**Bow(-ing)** 1. ___ in Japan shows respect. 2. The meaning of a ___ depends on the situation, depth, and length of time you hold it.
Buddhism 1. About 70% of the people of Japan practice ___. Many also practice Shinto. 2. Japan's two traditional religions are Shinto, the indigenous religion, and ___ which was introduced from the Asian mainland in the 6th century.	**Cherry Tree(s)** 1. ___ and their blossoms are called *sakura.* The Japanese Meteorological Agency tracks the front of their blossoming as it moves northward up the archipelago. 2. *Hanami* is the centuries-old practice of picnicking under a blooming *sakura,* or ___.
Chicamatsu Monzaemon 1. This dramatist lived from 1653 to 1725. 2. *Kikusenya Kassen,* or *Battles of the Kikusenya,* is his most famous work.	**Chrysanthemum Throne** 1. When___ is used to represent the Japanese monarchy, it is a metonymy.* 2. ___ can refer to specific seating or it can be an abstract concept representing the Japanese monarchy. *Metonymy: A figure of speech in which one word or phrase is substituted for another with which it is closely associated

Daimyo 1. The ___ were feudal lords. At one time a *samurai* became a ___ by controlling enough land to produce a *koku* of rice each year. 2. The ___ of the Tokugawa period differed from previous ones because they were virtually monarchs within their domains.	**Diet** 1. The bicameral legislature of Japan is called the National ___. 2. In addition to passing laws, the ___ selects the Prime Minister.
Edo 1. Tokugawa Ieyasu founded the Tokugawa, or ___, Shogunate. He chose ___ as Japan's new capital. 2. Until 1868 Tokyo was called ___.	**Emperor(s)** 1. Jimmu Tenno became Japan's first ___ in 660 BCE. 2. Akihito became ___ on January 7, 1989, after the death of his father, Hirohito.
Haiku 1. A ___ is a 17-syllable poem. 2. Matso Basho is famous for his ___ poetry.	**Hideki Tojo** 1. ___ was prime minister of Japan during World War II. 2. ___ was executed on December 23, 1948, for war crimes.
Hiroshima 1. On August 6, 1945, the United States used its atomic weapon against ___. 2. Three days after bombing ___, the United States bombed Nagasaki.	**Hokkaido** 1. ___ is the northernmost major island of Japan. 2. The Tsugaru Strait separates the island of ___ from the island of Honshu.
Honshu 1. ___ is Japan's largest island. Tokyo is on this island. 2. ___ is the main island of Japan. It is the seventh largest island in the world.	**Ikebana** 1. ___ is a popular form of Japanese flower arrangement. Emphasis is on shape, line, and form. 2. ___ means "living flowers." It is sometimes called *kado,* or "the way of flowers."
Japan Bingo	© Barbara M Peller

Imperial Palace 1. Edo Castle became the ___. 2. The ___ in Tokyo is the main residence of the Emperor of Japan.	**Kabuki** 1. ___ is a traditional Japanese popular drama with singing and dancing. 2. ___ combines music, dance, and mime.
Kamikaze(s) 1. During World War II ___ pilots were assigned to crash their plaines into their targets. 2. Literally, the word ___ means "divine wind."	**Kobe** 1. This port is the capital of Hyogo Prefecture on the southern side of the main island of Honshu. 2. ___, one of Japan's ten largest cities, is world famous for its local brand of beef.
Kyoto 1. ___ served as Japan's capital and the emperor's residence from 794 CE until 1868 CE. 2. Although no longer the capital of Japan, ___ is still Japan's religious center.	**Matso Basho** 1. This seventeenth-century poet is known for his haiku. 2. In "Oku no hosomichi," or "The Narrow Road to the Deep North," ___ describes his visit to northern Japan.
Meiji 1. Mutsuhito became known as Emperor ___. He moved from Kyoto to Tokyo, which became the new capital. 2. The ___ Era restored imperial rule. It lasted from 1868 CE to 1912 CE.	**Minamoto Yoritomo** 1. ___ was appointed *shogun* in 1192 CE and established the the first *bakufu,* or *shogunate.* 2. ___ was the founder and the first *shogun* of the Kamakura Shogunate of Japan. He ruled from 1192 to 1199.
Mount Fuji 1. At 12,388 feet, ___ is Japan's highest mountain. Its nearly perfect conical form is a favorite with artists and is considered the sacred symbol of Japan. 2. This dormant volcano is in central Honshu, about 60 miles west of Tokyo.	**Mount Misen** 1. ___ is the highest peak on the island of Itsukushima, commonly known as Miyajima. 2. Near the summit of ___ are several temple structures, including the *Reikado,* or Hall of the Spiritual Flame.

Nara 1. In 710 CE, ___ became the first permanent Japanese capital. 2. The capital was moved from ___ to Nagaoka and then to Heian-kyo, now central Kyoto.	**Oda Nobunaga** 1. This warrior was a member of the Fujiwara family. He overthrew the Ashikaga Shogunate and tried to unify Japan under his rule. 2. By the time of his death in 1582 CE, he had brought almost half of the provinces under his control. His successor, Toyotomi Hideyoshi, would unify all of Japan.
Okinawa 1. ___ is the southernmost prefecture in Japan. 2. After World War II, ___ was placed under United States administration, but in 1972 it was returned to Japan.	**Osaka** 1. Keihanshin is the second largest metropolitan area in Japan by population; it includes the metropolitan areas of ___, Kobe, and Kyoto. 2. ___ is the third largest city in Japan after Tokyo and Yokohama.
Pearl Harbor 1. The Imperial Japanese Navy made a surprise attack against the United States naval base at ___, Hawaii, on the morning of December 7, 1941. 2. The attack on ___ led to America's entry into World War II.	**Prefectures** 1. Japan is divided into 47 governmental units called ___. 2. Seven of the 8 general regions of Japan contain several ___; the Hokkaido region covers only Hokkaido.
Rice 1. The cultivation of ___ is very important in Japanese society. During the Edo period (1603–1868), salaries and wages were calculated in ___. 2. A *koku* is a unit of volume. It was originally defined as a specific amount of ___.	**Rim of Fire** 1. The Pacific ___ is an area where the movement of tectonic plates causes many earthquakes and volcanic eruptions. 2. Like other places within the Pacific ___, Japan has many earthquakes and volcanic eruptions.
Russo-Japanese War 1. The Battle of Tsushima Strait in May 1905 was the last battle of the ___. Japan was victorious in both the battle and the war. 2. The Treaty of Portsmouth ended the ___. Among other things, Japan's control of Korea was recognized. Japan Bingo	**Samurai** 1. These warriors made up the ruling military class. Their code was called, *bushido,* or "way of the warrior." 2. The ___ were skilled in the use of many weapons, but they were best known for their skill with their swords.

Sea of Japan 1. The ___ is between the Asian mainland and the Japanese archipelago. 2. The ___ is bordered by Japan, North Korea, Russia and South Korea.	**Shinto** 1. ___, the indigenous religion of Japan, is based upon devotion to invisible spiritual beings and powers called *kami*. 2. ___ is the native religion of Japan. Local shrines are especially important.
Shogun(s) 1. ___ were military rulers. They ruled from the 1300s to 1868, when the emperors again gained power. 2. Minamoto Yoritomo was appointed *shogun* in 1192 and established the the first *bakufu,* or *shogunate.*	**Taika Reforms** 1. The ___ were a set of political established by Emperor Kotoku in 645 CE to enhance the power of the imperial court. 2. Prince Nakano-Oe, who became Emperor Tenji, and Nakatomi Kamatari were responsible for the ___ of 645.
Tokugawa Ieyasu 1. Born Matsudaira Takechiy, ___ was the founder of the last *shogunate* in Japan. In 1603 Emperor Go-YMzei, ruler only in name, gave him the historic title of *shogun.* 2. The mausoleum of this warrior and statesman at Nikko is one of the most important shrines in Japan.	**Tokyo** 1. ___ is the capital of Japan. 2. The Ginza is an upscale area of ___ with many high-end stores. It is named after the silver-coin mint established there in 1612 CE during the Edo period.
Toyotomi Hideyoshi 1. ___ was Oda Nobunaga's successor; he completed the unification of Japan begun by Oda Nobunaga. 2. After his death in 1598, his policies of national unification were followed by Tokugawa Ieyasu.	**Tsunami(s)** 1. Undersea earthquakes make the Japanese coastline vulnerable to danger from ___. 2. On March 11, 2011, a devastating 9.0 earthquake triggered a powerful 30-foot ___. It set off a nuclear crisis.
Wabi-sabi 1. ___ means "less is more." 2. ___ is a world view based on the acceptance of the imperfection of nature and the appreciation of things as they are. It is the acceptance of the natural cycle of growth, decay, and death.	**Yokohama** 1. ___ is the second largest city after Tokyo. 2. It is the Japan's largest port and an important manufacturing and shipbuilding center.

Japan Bingo

Japan Bingo

Rim of Fire	Ainu	Asia	Honshu	Bonsai
Hiroshima	Archipelago	Tsunami(s)	Mount Misen	Sea of Japan
Toyotomi Hideyoshi	Mount Fuji		Pearl Harbor	Wabi-sabi
Tokyo	Samurai	Tokugawa Ieyasu	Minamoto Yoritomo	Oda Nobunaga
Osaka	Kabuki	Emperor(s)	Shogun(s)	Kyoto

Japan Bingo: Card No. 1

Japan
Bingo

Tokyo	Toyotomi Hideyoshi	Kobe	Russo-Japanese War	Meiji
Oda Nobunaga	Haiku	Cherry Tree(s)	Samurai	Okinawa
Chrysanthemum Throne	Kabuki		Kamikaze(s)	Tokugawa Ieyasu
Prefectures	Rice	Mount Fuji	Yokohama	Bonsai
Sea of Japan	Tsunami(s)	Emperor(s)	Hiroshima	Shogun(s)

Japan Bingo

Kabuki	Tokugawa Ieyasu	Haiku	Minamoto Yoritomo	Toyotomi Hideyoshi
Oda Nobunaga	Archipelago	Chicamatsu Monzaemon	Ainu	Imperial Palace
Samurai	Tsunami(s)		Okinawa	Bakufu
Mount Fuji	Chrysanthemum Throne	Osaka	Prefectures	Kobe
Shogun(s)	Daimyo	Emperor(s)	Yokohama	Meiji

Japan Bingo: Card No. 3

Japan Bingo

Mount Fuji	Okinawa	Asia	Daimyo	Meiji
Nara	Buddhism	Ainu	Russo-Japanese War	Toyotomi Hideyoshi
Pearl Harbor	Prefectures		Kyoto	Honshu
Tokugawa Ieyasu	Archipelago	Tsunami(s)	Emperor(s)	Cherry Tree(s)
Diet	Sea of Japan	Bow(-ing)	Shogun(s)	Wabi-sabi

Japan Bingo

Sea of Japan	Bonsai	Samurai	Cherry Tree(s)	Daimyo
Nara	Tokugawa Ieyasu	Chicamatsu Monzaemon	Kamikaze(s)	Archipelago
Asia	Wabi-sabi		Mount Misen	Ikebana
Kyoto	Meiji	Rim of Fire	Yokohama	Edo
Haiku	Emperor(s)	Toyotomi Hideyoshi	Mount Fuji	Pearl Harbor

Japan Bingo: Card No. 5

Japan Bingo

Bakufu	Okinawa	Kobe	Meiji	Wabi-sabi
Minamoto Yoritomo	Samurai	Edo	Ainu	Toyotomi Hideyoshi
Russo-Japanese War	Diet		Buddhism	Kamikaze(s)
Emperor(s)	Osaka	Yokohama	Bow(-ing)	Asia
Oda Nobunaga	Cherry Tree(s)	Rim of Fire	Pearl Harbor	Hideki Tojo

Japan Bingo

Rim of Fire	Okinawa	Ikebana	Tokugawa Ieyasu	Haiku
Oda Nobunaga	Meiji	Kabuki	Archipelago	Nara
Wabi-sabi	Honshu		Kamikaze(s)	Buddhism
Mount Fuji	Prefectures	Chicamatsu Monzaemon	Tokyo	Chrysanthemum Throne
Emperor(s)	Daimyo	Yokohama	Bow(-ing)	Bakufu

Japan Bingo

Pearl Harbor	Okinawa	Hokkaido	Minamoto Yoritomo	Buddhism
Nara	Asia	Russo-Japanese War	Wabi-sabi	Cherry Tree(s)
Hideki Tojo	Daimyo		Meiji	Bonsai
Shogun(s)	Mount Fuji	Tokyo	Diet	Prefectures
Tsunami(s)	Emperor(s)	Bow(-ing)	Samurai	Oda Nobunaga

Japan Bingo

Kamikaze(s)	Haiku	Kabuki	Hideki Tojo	Daimyo
Diet	Meiji	Pearl Harbor	Samurai	Okinawa
Imperial Palace	Rim of Fire		Archipelago	Hokkaido
Edo	Bonsai	Osaka	Mount Misen	Ikebana
Prefectures	Yokohama	Chicamatsu Monzaemon	Tokyo	Kyoto

Japan Bingo: Card No. 9

Japan Bingo

Tokyo	Minamoto Yoritomo	Buddhism	Russo-Japanese War	Hideki Tojo
Wabi-sabi	Cherry Tree(s)	Ainu	Archipelago	Meiji
Daimyo	Okinawa		Honshu	Chrysanthemum Throne
Osaka	Kyoto	Edo	Yokohama	Imperial Palace
Chicamatsu Monzaemon	Oda Nobunaga	Kobe	Sea of Japan	Pearl Harbor

Japan Bingo: Card No. 10

Japan Bingo

Bakufu	Okinawa	Samurai	Edo	Oda Nobunaga
Hokkaido	Imperial Palace	Mount Misen	Kamikaze(s)	Ainu
Nara	Meiji		Kobe	Kabuki
Chicamatsu Monzaemon	Toyotomi Hideyoshi	Yokohama	Daimyo	Tokyo
Diet	Emperor(s)	Rim of Fire	Bow(-ing)	Haiku

Japan Bingo

Haiku	Bonsai	Imperial Palace	Minamoto Yoritomo	Kamikaze(s)
Kabuki	Oda Nobunaga	Asia	Bow(-ing)	Archipelago
Rim of Fire	Ikebana		Wabi-sabi	Russo-Japanese War
Emperor(s)	Prefectures	Meiji	Tokyo	Nara
Okinawa	Hokkaido	Daimyo	Diet	Cherry Tree(s)

Japan Bingo

Edo	Bonsai	Bakufu	Imperial Palace	Wabi-sabi
Asia	Hokkaido	Meiji	Kamikaze(s)	Chrysanthemum Throne
Minamoto Yoritomo	Cherry Tree(s)		Kabuki	Ikebana
Pearl Harbor	Yokohama	Buddhism	Daimyo	Tokyo
Emperor(s)	Kyoto	Bow(-ing)	Rim of Fire	Mount Misen

Japan Bingo: Card No. 13

Japan
Bingo

Hiroshima	Meiji	Samurai	Kamikaze(s)	Diet
Cherry Tree(s)	Rim of Fire	Imperial Palace	Archipelago	Okinawa
Edo	Honshu		Kobe	Chicamatsu Monzaemon
Kyoto	Yokohama	Daimyo	Buddhism	Bakufu
Emperor(s)	Russo-Japanese War	Chrysanthemum Throne	Oda Nobunaga	Pearl Harbor

Japan Bingo

Mount Misen	Kamikaze(s)	Samurai	Haiku	Minamoto Yoritomo
Bakufu	Kobe	Ainu	Asia	Diet
Wabi-sabi	Rim of Fire		Toyotomi Hideyoshi	Okinawa
Emperor(s)	Imperial Palace	Hokkaido	Yokohama	Edo
Oda Nobunaga	Prefectures	Bow(-ing)	Hideki Tojo	Kabuki

Japan Bingo

Buddhism	Imperial Palace	Hokkaido	Hideki Tojo	Rice
Russo-Japanese War	Chrysanthemum Throne	Ikebana	Nara	Honshu
Edo	Bonsai		Wabi-sabi	Kabuki
Mount Fuji	Cherry Tree(s)	Emperor(s)	Mount Misen	Tokyo
Diet	Taika Reforms	Bow(-ing)	Prefectures	Okinawa

Japan Bingo: Card No. 16

Japan Bingo

Chicamatsu Monzaemon	Shinto	Matso Basho	Imperial Palace	Hiroshima
Mount Misen	Diet	Yokohama	Honshu	Ikebana
Kamikaze(s)	Pearl Harbor		Taika Reforms	Hokkaido
Kyoto	Oda Nobunaga	Tokyo	Samurai	Chrysanthemum Throne
Osaka	Edo	Haiku	Minamoto Yoritomo	Bonsai

Japan Bingo

Hideki Tojo	Daimyo	Cherry Tree(s)	Edo	Russo-Japanese War
Okinawa	Chicamatsu Monzaemon	Osaka	Wabi-sabi	Diet
Kamikaze(s)	Chrysanthemum Throne		Matso Basho	Asia
Bonsai	Ainu	Yokohama	Tokyo	Kobe
Taika Reforms	Imperial Palace	Samurai	Shinto	Bakufu

Japan Bingo

Wabi-sabi	Bakufu	Imperial Palace	Hokkaido	Tokyo
Mount Misen	Minamoto Yoritomo	Okinawa	Haiku	Honshu
Shinto	Daimyo		Archipelago	Toyotomi Hideyoshi
Kobe	Taika Reforms	Osaka	Prefectures	Matso Basho
Asia	Rice	Oda Nobunaga	Pearl Harbor	Bow(-ing)

Japan Bingo

Hiroshima	Shinto	Minamoto Yoritomo	Imperial Palace	Bow(-ing)
Cherry Tree(s)	Kabuki	Nara	Osaka	Russo-Japanese War
Bonsai	Ikebana		Mount Fuji	Ainu
Sea of Japan	Tsunami(s)	Shogun(s)	Prefectures	Taika Reforms
Tokugawa Ieyasu	Pearl Harbor	Rice	Tokyo	Matso Basho

Japan Bingo

Mount Misen	Bakufu	Nara	Imperial Palace	Sea of Japan
Bonsai	Matso Basho	Buddhism	Hokkaido	Rim of Fire
Chrysanthemum Throne	Oda Nobunaga		Shinto	Samurai
Osaka	Haiku	Taika Reforms	Kyoto	Pearl Harbor
Mount Fuji	Rice	Bow(-ing)	Chicamatsu Monzaemon	Prefectures

Japan Bingo

Hideki Tojo	Kobe	Matso Basho	Asia	Edo
Russo-Japanese War	Minamoto Yoritomo	Toyotomi Hideyoshi	Hokkaido	Archipelago
Cherry Tree(s)	Honshu		Rim of Fire	Ikebana
Taika Reforms	Kyoto	Prefectures	Ainu	Nara
Rice	Chicamatsu Monzaemon	Shinto	Chrysanthemum Throne	Mount Fuji

Japan Bingo

Buddhism	Shinto	Haiku	Asia	Bow(-ing)
Bakufu	Hiroshima	Oda Nobunaga	Mount Misen	Ainu
Kobe	Edo		Shogun(s)	Rim of Fire
Chrysanthemum Throne	Rice	Taika Reforms	Chicamatsu Monzaemon	Prefectures
Sea of Japan	Tsunami(s)	Pearl Harbor	Osaka	Matso Basho

Japan Bingo

Buddhism	Pearl Harbor	Hiroshima	Shinto	Hokkaido
Matso Basho	Bow(-ing)	Nara	Russo-Japanese War	Rim of Fire
Ikebana	Hideki Tojo		Edo	Chrysanthemum Throne
Sea of Japan	Shogun(s)	Taika Reforms	Chicamatsu Monzaemon	Bonsai
Tokugawa Ieyasu	Mount Fuji	Rice	Minamoto Yoritomo	Tsunami(s)

Japan Bingo

Mount Fuji	Nara	Shinto	Samurai	Matso Basho
Ainu	Bonsai	Mount Misen	Buddhism	Archipelago
Kyoto	Hokkaido		Shogun(s)	Taika Reforms
Toyotomi Hideyoshi	Sea of Japan	Tsunami(s)	Rice	Honshu
Bow(-ing)	Hiroshima	Cherry Tree(s)	Diet	Tokugawa Ieyasu

Japan Bingo: Card No. 25

Japan Bingo

Matso Basho	Shinto	Kobe	Russo-Japanese War	Hideki Tojo
Osaka	Minamoto Yoritomo	Hokkaido	Hiroshima	Buddhism
Kyoto	Shogun(s)		Honshu	Mount Fuji
Chicamatsu Monzaemon	Asia	Sea of Japan	Rice	Taika Reforms
Ikebana	Diet	Samurai	Tsunami(s)	Tokugawa Ieyasu

Japan Bingo: Card No. 26

Japan Bingo

Kobe	Cherry Tree(s)	Shinto	Hiroshima	Kabuki
Sea of Japan	Shogun(s)	Mount Misen	Taika Reforms	Archipelago
Yokohama	Tsunami(s)		Rice	Mount Fuji
Hideki Tojo	Bakufu	Nara	Tokugawa Ieyasu	Ainu
Diet	Honshu	Matso Basho	Toyotomi Hideyoshi	Ikebana

Japan Bingo: Card No. 27

Japan Bingo

Kobe	Hiroshima	Toyotomi Hideyoshi	Shinto	Buddhism
Kabuki	Matso Basho	Shogun(s)	Russo-Japanese War	Honshu
Tsunami(s)	Chrysanthemum Throne		Ikebana	Osaka
Tokyo	Hideki Tojo	Oda Nobunaga	Rice	Taika Reforms
Asia	Kamikaze(s)	Diet	Tokugawa Ieyasu	Sea of Japan

Japan Bingo

Matso Basho	Hiroshima	Hideki Tojo	Mount Misen	Kamikaze(s)
Prefectures	Osaka	Nara	Ikebana	Toyotomi Hideyoshi
Kyoto	Shogun(s)		Archipelago	Shinto
Kabuki	Sea of Japan	Meiji	Rice	Taika Reforms
Buddhism	Hokkaido	Tokugawa Ieyasu	Bakufu	Tsunami(s)

Japan Bingo

Daimyo	Shinto	Russo-Japanese War	Kamikaze(s)	Taika Reforms
Ainu	Hiroshima	Kobe	Honshu	Archipelago
Kyoto	Edo		Ikebana	Nara
Tokugawa Ieyasu	Bakufu	Asia	Rice	Shogun(s)
Sea of Japan	Wabi-sabi	Tsunami(s)	Matso Basho	Toyotomi Hideyoshi

Japan Bingo: Card No. 30

www.ingramcontent.com/pod-product-compliance
Lightning Source LLC
LaVergne TN
LVHW061338060426

835511LV00014B/1981